Networking

Networking

How to Creatively Tap Your People Resources

by Colleen S. Clarke

SkillPath Publications

Mission, Kansas

Editor: Kelly Scanlon

Cover Design: Rod Hankins

Page Layout: Becky Robinette

Library of Congress Catalog Card Number: 95-71726

ISBN: 1-878542-41-9

10   9   8   7   6   04   05

Printed in the United States of America

*To the members of the Executive Advancement
Resource Network (E.A.R.N.)*

"Regardless of what it is you're networking for, approach it with enthusiasm so as to enroll people in your vision. People are naturally drawn to others with a clear vision. They want to be a part of your positive energy. Put it out in a positive way; then stand back and wait for it to come to you."

Leslie Knight
Director
Technical Service Council of Canada

Contents

Preface

I've been networking most of my life it seems. Of course, I didn't realize it until the late '80s when the word finally made its way into our vocabulary. Because I've lived in a few different cities, often not knowing anyone when I first arrived, I've had to do a lot of information seeking just to get myself established with the necessities of life (doctors, hairdressers, dry cleaners, shopping centers, etc.), let alone in order to find a new job or a place to live.

I get such pleasure out of connecting people to people that I look for opportunities to do so if one hasn't presented itself for a while.

A friend of mine asked how I could stay in touch with so many people throughout North America and why. First, people's lives fascinate me. Second, people need people. You just never know when you might want to take a holiday somewhere or be able to refer someone to someone else. Networking takes time and energy galore, but the rewards are monumental.

At one point in my career, for example, I decided I wanted to make a career change but stay within the industry I know, shopping centers. Retail leasing was unfamiliar to me, and I was uncertain about whether this was the area I really wanted to pursue because marketing and promotions had been my forté for eight years.

I called a couple of friends who were working in retail leasing and pumped them for specific information about the work. What was a typical day like? What skills did a person need to be successful and to enjoy the job? How was the market right now? What were some of the prominent companies involved in leasing? Would my knowledge and somewhat related experience be enough to allow me to make a change?

These people gave me the names of key players in the industry—the decision makers. (I call decision makers Category "A" networking contacts.) I arranged information meetings with two or three directors and asked them similar questions, not once showing any interest one way or the other or asking for a job. Each contact represented a different market and demographic, which gave me a sense of comparison.

Much to my surprise, one of the companies called me within two weeks to interview with their leasing department. Less than a week later, I was offered a job. The other contacts I had made while I was gathering information formed my immediate network within this new industry, and at association meetings and conventions, I already knew the competition. My contacts, in turn, felt comfortable introducing me to the regional and national retailers I would be doing business with down the road. I was in!

This particular episode drove home to me the importance of a network, not to mention the importance of a network within the job itself.

Where networking really came to the forefront for me was when I started a networking support group for unemployed business professionals when I found myself unemployed during the recession of the early '90s. My idea was to get some people together to share contacts, ideas, and leads. I thought that if we could support one another, maybe we'd fare this period more easily and find jobs more quickly.

The result was E.A.R.N., the Executive Advancement Resource Network, which is Canada's first and largest self-help networking group for professionals in career transition.

Currently, over 2,000 people have attended a weekly E.A.R.N. meeting since its inception in October 1990. The whole premise of the group is networking—for participants to tell as many people as possible the kind of work they are looking for and to ask whether others in the group know someone who may be able to help them.

Hundreds of people who had never so much as asked for directions are approaching perfect strangers every week, anxious to give and get help from fifty to eighty-five of the most diverse individuals you'll ever meet in one room.

Yes, people are getting jobs, finding roommates and places to live, making lifelong friends, going into business together, and stretching and growing like they never thought they could do, not in a million years.

The purpose of this little book is to introduce you to the concepts of networking and to make you feel comfortable with the process. The four major areas we will look at are:

1. The barriers to networking

2. Networking etiquette

3. Improving your networking skills

4. The Advice Call, with a script that will allow you to say, "It works!"

Have fun, learn, stretch, and grow. Dare to risk and, of course, set a goal. Before you know it, you will be a resource person to all your friends and business acquaintances.

You alone can do it, but you can't do it alone!

Best regards,

Colleen S. Clarke

CHAPTER 1

Networking: Not Just a Buzzword of the Nineties

"Knowledgeable people know facts. Successful people and prosperous people know people."

John Demartini

Networking is not just a buzzword of the nineties. People have been networking since the beginning of time. It's just that the term "networking" didn't come into vogue until the 1980s.

You've obviously heard something about networking and decided that you're ready and willing to take the plunge to make it an active part of your life. First, you should know that you are really going to enjoy the process. You see, anyone can network. You do it already, every day of your life—but you just don't know it.

Have you ever moved to a new town or city? Started a new job at a new company? Had children? Then at one time or another, you've probably asked someone for *advice, information,* an *opinion,* a *suggestion,* or *help.* Have you asked for the name of a hairdresser, where the local mall is, for a stock tip, or for career assistance? You have? Then you've networked!

Men have been networking for eons. You may have heard of the "good-old-boy network." Men seldom think twice about calling up a golf buddy, business acquaintance, or client to get the scoop on a new stock, check the credit rating of a new client, or find a secretary or new job.

Women on the other hand, says Mary Scott Welch in her book *Networking: The Great New Way For Women to Get Ahead,* sometimes have trouble asking for and expecting help. Yet they are terrific at *eliciting* information. How many times have you heard women ask for a recipe, the name of someone's real estate agent, or where to find a good nanny for the kids?

The Networking Exchange

Networking is the art of creatively and resourcefully tapping the market of "people resources" available to you, people who can help you in all or any aspect of your life—career, business, or personal. According to Anthony Putnam, author of *Marketing Your Services,* the purpose of networking is "to give and to get information. If you use networking properly, nobody feels pressured or used or put on the spot. You are not *selling.* You are *telling.* You are not asking for favors; you are giving valuable information."

Networking is, quite simply, an *exchange* of information, services, or resources among individuals, groups, or associations. What people who network regularly have found is that it is an educational and time- and energy-saving process for *getting* the information they want or need and for establishing contacts. Networking also provides the opportunity to *give* expertise or knowledge.

Remember this: the key word to networking is *exchange*.

Why Network?

Maybe you're the kind of person who needs a logical reason for doing or trying something new. If so, you will want to know why you should network and what you can get out of a networking consultation. You will:

1. Further your existing market research.
2. Acquire names of additional resources you can call or visit.
3. Gain confidence.
4. Learn new skills.
5. Increase your self-esteem.
6. Meet new people and make new friends.

Networking means getting your face in front of as many people as possible—meeting the decision-makers in order to personalize your capabilities, sell a product, or be remembered the next time. Your chances of being chosen for an important project or getting the best deal you can possibly negotiate will come your way more easily and more quickly if people can see your image before them.

To win in today's world, you must be constantly looking for business and personal contacts and take advantage of opportunities when they occur. Did you know, for example, that:

- A referral generates 80 percent more results than a cold call?
- Most people you meet have at least 100 contacts?
- Anyone you might want to meet or contact is only four to five people away from you?

With more and more people starting home-based businesses or consultancy practices, *personal exposure* to potential customers is vital. And consider this: Eighty percent of the jobs available are found through the *hidden job market*. How do you successfully access the hidden job market? Through networking, of course.

Opportunities advertised in the newspaper draw, on average, 400 to 800 responses. When your resume arrives on a recruiter's desk, it is just another piece of paper that has to be screened before a decision is made about who to hire. There is no warm body to go with that paper, no award-winning smile, no subtle humor. How accurately can someone identify four or five of the best applicants to interview based on a few words written on a sheet of paper, often by someone other than the applicant? On the other hand, wouldn't you rather be one of only three or four applicants being considered for a position? You can be if you use networking to access the hidden job market.

Your first and possibly only contact with the recruiter or decision maker is the one you make personally, through a referral or on your own. Maybe the rapport you establish with that person or the skills you have to offer are so impressive (not to mention the impression you'll make by taking the initiative to make the contact in the first place) that your contact will decide to create a position for you.

You can see for yourself how powerful networking can be.

Networking Tips

Here are some tips to keep in mind as you begin your networking experience:

1. Make networking ongoing.
2. Treat any contact with respect, and be businesslike even if that person is a friend.
3. Ask whether you can use your referral's name when you follow up on a lead your referral gives you.
4. Be dependable and reliable.
5. Give your "sales pitch" in 50 words or less.
6. Learn to listen and retain information.
7. Be yourself.
8. Blow your own whistle.

As you network, remember that it requires:

1. A clear goal.
2. Solid planning.
3. Organization.
4. Energy.

5. Imagination.
6. A willingness to stretch and grow.

And sometimes even guts!

No doubt about it, networking takes time and patience as well as positive energy and a confident attitude. It demands creating a clear vision and plan of what you want to find out. Getting information from people and using it wisely can help you become more clearly focused and take more control of your career direction and other life choices. You will be able to make wiser decisions and find the solution that is best for you at the time—often saving time, energy, and money, not to mention aggravation.

CHAPTER 2

Establishing Your Networking Goals

"The longest journey begins with a single step."

Confucius

Goals give your life meaning and direction. Without specific goals, including setting a date by which you will accomplish them, there's little point to networking. Use Exercise 1 to begin establishing some of your networking goals.

■ EXERCISE 1:
Establishing Your Networking Goals

1. Place a check next to the statements that describe the goals you wish to attain:

   ❏   To change jobs soon

   ❏   To make a complete career change

   ❏   To increase my knowledge and expertise in my field of work

   ❏   To make my skills and expertise more visible to others

   ❏   To generate new business and professional contacts

   ❏   To make new friends

   ❏   To find a new service or product

2. My specific networking goal is:

   _____

   _____

   _____

   _____

3. The date by which I will accomplish my goal is:

   _____

Self-Assessment and Goal Achievement

Now that you have identified your goals, the next step is to inventory your personal resources; that is, to identify the skills, strengths and weaknesses, values, and qualities that you have that can help you achieve your networking goals. An excellent workbook to assist you with this self-assessment process is *The Career Discovery Process* by Gerald Sturman, Ph.D. During this period of self-assessment, truly try to get to know yourself better.

Skills. Your skills are the things that you do well—communicate effectively, operate a computer, design clothing, work with numbers, negotiate, delegate, write creatively, or speak two languages.

Networking effectively requires a combination of people skills. According to Venda Raye-Johnson, author of *Effective Networking*, these six skills are vital to strategic networking:

1. *Asserting yourself positively*
   - Don't apologize for asking for help.
   - Take the initiative in offering help.
   - Don't compare yourself to others.
   - Accept rejections as part of being assertive.
   - Look your best so you can feel and, therefore, act your best.

2. *Asking good questions*
   - Know your goals before your meeting.
   - Prepare your questions beforehand.
   - Use open-ended questions.
   - Know what it is you would like to get from the meeting.

3. *Listening with your "third" ear*
   - Listen to the total person. Be an "active listener."
   - Listen to what is spoken and what is not spoken.
   - Listen for cues to feelings and meanings.
   - Demonstrate acceptance and interest in the speaker.
   - Reciprocate with good questions.

4. *Presenting yourself attractively*
   - Ninety percent of how you present yourself is done visually; 10 percent is done verbally.

5. *Being viewed as knowledgeable or skillful in a particular area*
   - You have skills, talents, and abilities to offer. What is your niche or area of excellence?

6. *Showing interest in empowering others*
   - Display genuine interest and a helpful attitude.
   - Show and tell people they are valued.
   - Listen to them.

EXERCISE 2:

Rating Your Networking Skills

A. Rate yourself on a scale of 1 to 5 on each of the following networking skills, with 5 being the highest.

1._____ I assert myself positively.

2._____ I ask good open-ended questions.

3._____ I understand what is being spoken and what is not being spoken.

4._____ I present myself attractively.

5._____ I am viewed as knowledgeable or skillful in a particular area.

6._____ I show interest in empowering others.

B. In which areas did you achieve an excellent rating (score of 4 or 5)?

_____

_____

C. Which areas need some fine-tuning (score of 3)? How can I accomplish this?

_____

_____

_____

D. Which areas are underdeveloped (score of 1 or 2)? Who could help me? Where can I go for help?

_____

_____

_____

To acquire and hone effective networking skills, you will constantly be on a campaign of self-growth and development—taking courses, reading self-help books, and broadening your comfort zone by stretching and growing at every opportunity.

Now that you have identified your skills, focus on your strengths, values, and qualities.

Strengths. Your *strengths* are the things that you *have*—patience, understanding, creativity, aptness.

Values. *Values* are often ignored in the self-assessment identification process, but they are vitally important. Values are the beliefs you hold dear, your morals, the things that are important to you in life— putting in a good day's work, being rewarded for a job well done, working in a harmonious environment, or empowering and coaching a team.

Qualities. Last, but not least, are *qualities,* your personality traits— assertiveness, perseverance, stick-to-it-iveness, helpfulness, kindness, thoughtfulness, selflessness.

█ EXERCISE 3:

Take a few minutes to jot down your strongest strengths, values, and personal qualities.

Strengths	Values	Qualities

Now, take what you have learned about yourself during this assessment process and determine the best strategies for achieving the particular networking goals you have established. For example, if you wrote down that you have an excellent telephone presence and skills, you may want to consider using the telephone as a primary networking tool. Or, if you listed your time as something that you value, you may want to consider networking methods and events that are very focused rather than leisurely.

You can't effectively use networking strategies that you are uncomfortable with or that are incongruent with your personal qualities.

Remember, too, that a network is a tool. You will want to create a network that is the best tool possible for achieving your particular goal. You wouldn't use a paintbrush to write a letter; you'd use a pen. Likewise, it may not be appropriate to use your professional business contacts for achieving personal or social goals. And don't settle for a generalist as a contact when you need to obtain information about a specific issue or product. Instead, create a network that consists of specialists in that area. If, for example, your goal is to move from accounting into human resources, you will have to broaden your immediate network to include people—such as the director of human resources at your company—who are already in positions relating to your goal. These individuals can put you in touch with like-minded associates, people with different skills, experiences, and expertise than what you possess.

Two other powerful devices you can use to accomplish your goals through networking are:

1. *Visualization.* Visualize what you will look like and feel like once you have succeeded. It may mean altering your self-image, but visualization is an incredibly strong method of acquiring what you want in life.

2. *Mentoring.* A mentor is a person you trust and who has been or is where you want to be. Having a mentor involves give and take. When you've networked your goal, make yourself available as a mentor.

Networking that is goal-driven allows you to work smarter, not harder. You may spend some extra time up front establishing your goals, but in the long run, you'll spend less time spinning your wheels and changing directions because your path will be focused.

CHAPTER 3

Your Contact Network

"We act, behave and feel according to what we consider our self-image to be and we do not deviate from the pattern."

Dr. Maxwell Maltz

Bob had recently graduated from a computer training program at a local college but was having trouble finding a job through the traditional method of answering newspaper ads. After his family encouraged him to try networking, Bob signed up for career counseling.

After several sessions, a family member referred him to a company that needed some temporary help with its ancient computer system. Bob's counselor mentioned that she knew an individual named Ahmed who repaired computers and would probably be available for consultation if Bob felt he'd gotten in over his head.

Bob took the initiative to visit Ahmed to establish a personal contact before starting the new job. Bob mentioned that if he needed to buy some parts down the line, he'd keep Ahmed in mind.

Later, Ahmed told the counselor that Bob had stopped by for some instruction and had also mentioned buying some parts from him, a benefit Ahmed had not expected.

"Network, network, network!" exclaimed the counselor.

"Is that networking?" asked Ahmed. "I thought networking only existed for computers!"

This story illustrates the concept of *contact networking*—of using people you already know or people your friends and associates know in order to achieve a goal. Consider how many people benefited in the example. Bob found a job. The company received desperately needed help with its computer system. And Ahmed found a new outlet for selling computer parts. Talk about a win-win situation for everyone involved!

Notice that all of this came about through referrals from people Bob and Ahmed already knew—their family and friends. Many people think that networking means handing out business cards at so-called "networking functions." That is one type of networking. But the vast majority of networking that takes place each day is among people you already know.

Consider your contacts in each of the following areas, and then use Exercise 4 to write them down. You'll probably be surprised at just how many contacts you already have.

Informal Contacts

- Relatives
- Friends
- Neighbors
- Club members
- People you've met while traveling
- Acquaintances
- People you've met socially or at sporting events
- People you've met while doing volunteer work
- People you ride the elevator with

Educational Contacts

- People from school or college
- Parents of your children's friends
- Teachers or professors
- Professional associations

Formal Contacts

- Co-workers
- Salespeople
- Consultants
- Lawyers, accountants
- Former employers
- Doctors, dentists
- Hairdressers, stylists, manicurists, masseuses
- Real estate agents

Other Contacts

- Bank manager, tellers
- Community, business, government, political leaders
- Church members, pastors, ministers, rabbis
- Garage mechanics

■ EXERCISE 4:

Identifying Your Contact Network

Comprise a list of contacts you already have. As you prepare the list, don't discount anyone—put down any name that comes to mind. Prioritize the list only when you have finished writing down everyone you can think of. Consider these categories especially:

- People to whom you have easy access
- People who are knowledgeable in the areas you are pursuing
- People who know many other people

Your list will begin to grow extensively and quickly when you start the networking process and begin to accumulate referrals. Add lines as your network grows.

Doctor/dentist

_____

_____

Past associates

_____

_____

_____

Insurance/real estate agents

_____

_____

Friends

_____

_____

_____

Hairdressers

_____

_____

Business associates

_____

_____

Neighbors

_____

_____

Club/association members

_____

_____

Business owners

_____

_____

Bankers

_____

_____

Fellow volunteer workers

_____

_____

Relatives

_____

_____

Clergy

_____

_____

People I've met while traveling

_____

_____

Clients

_____

_____

Lawyers/accountants

_____

_____

The parents of your children's friends

_____

_____

Former employers

_____

_____

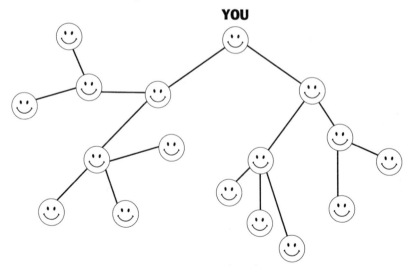

Your contact network grows exponentially
with every contact you make.

CHAPTER 4

Barriers to Networking

"For the first time in my life, after a 25-year career, I lost my job. I first heard about networking through my career counselor. She told me that the way to find a job today was through the hidden job market, which is uncovered through networking. Not having been in sales or marketing and uncomfortable with selling myself, I was nervous and scared about looking for a job in this way. Now I know better and realize that if I had been networking while I was still employed, doing it when I lost my job would have been so much easier. But, I learned the lesson too late. I own a retail franchise business now and talking to customers and new people I meet is my way of networking, daily...next time, I'll be prepared for whatever comes my way."

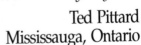

Ted Pittard
Mississauga, Ontario

Adapting to the fast pace of the twenty-first century will require an open mind, a certain amount of risk-taking, constantly upgrading your skills and training, and becoming more of a specialist in a generalist's world.

Don't let your fear of networking keep you from moving forward, from acting on an idea, or from improving a situation. People have been asking for *advice, information, opinions* (usually offered, not solicited), *help,* and *suggestions* with personal and business situations since the beginning of time. How do you think Christopher Columbus, an Italian, knew to ask Queen Isabella, a Spaniard, to finance his trip to the New World? He asked around, of course. He networked!

Here are some of the reasons, or excuses, people give most often for not networking:

1. *I don't have any contacts.* You only need to know one person to start networking. Consider that most people know between 100 to 1,000 people. You can generate a potential base of 200 to 2,000 leads from knowing only two people.

2. *I don't like having other people solve my problems.* You're not asking anyone to solve your problems, let alone to make decisions for you. Collect the information you acquire from various sources to make your own decisions and to formulate your plans.

3. *It will appear as if I'm begging.* Whatever you do, do not beg! To achieve the best results, ask for help, information, advice, or an opinion. Believe it or not, people love to give their opinion and are complimented when asked for advice.

4. *I don't like to use people.* Remember that networking is an exchange. Try to give back more than you get. View yourself as a resource person. You, too, have something to offer. It may be down the road, but you'll still be contributing. Build up your references so that eventually people seek you out for information or assistance.

5. *I will owe too many favors.* A genuine thank you is all most people ask in exchange for their expertise. A nice card or letter goes a long way and costs relatively nothing in terms of time or money. Look for opportunities and ways to return a favor.

6. *I feel uncomfortable networking and I lack confidence.* Change your attitude about what networking is. Set a clear goal, follow your plan, practice, and loosen up. Have fun with it. Don't look at networking as the "be all and end all." (Remember, too, that everyone puts his or her pants on one leg at a time.)

7. *I don't know what to say.* A script has been included in Chapter 7 to help you through some of your networking situations. Make sure you are well-prepared, and practice, practice, practice!

8. *I hate making cold calls.* Make them warm calls! Call only the people who have been referred to you by your initial contacts. When you say, "Hi, Mary Smith. My name is Bob Green. Jane Doe suggested I give you a call," you instantly build rapport with your contact. Send a letter beforehand so that when you call the contact, you can say, "He's expecting my call."

9. *No one can help me. Why should they?* Because people just naturally like to help. You do, don't you? So why wouldn't other people? Helping someone else makes most people feel good. Unless a person is truly too busy, doesn't have the expertise you thought, or is just plain uncooperative, you'll get all the assistance you'll need in most cases, and probably more.

10. *It doesn't work.* Have you ever decided to go on a holiday to a new destination where you didn't know the local accommodations or what the area had to offer? By sharing her tentative plans with others, one woman landed herself and her husband a free time-share with maps and recreational information galore.

    Also consider that a 1988 U.S. Department of Labor report stated that 85 percent of jobs were obtained that year through contacting employers directly or through individuals' own networks.

    Still think that networking doesn't work?

11. *I don't know how or where to start.* By the time you finish reading this book, you will be ready to conquer previously uncharted venues.

12. *I don't have enough time.* You'll find that networking actually saves an inordinate amount of time. Isn't it quicker to ask directions to the hardware section of a five-level department store than to wander around aimlessly guessing where it might be? Also, once your own resource base grows, you'll find that all it takes is one, maybe two calls, to find exactly what it is you need.

13. *I'm shy.* You won't be by the time you've made ten or twenty calls and talked to a few dozen people you've never set eyes on before. This is an excellent time to grow and stretch beyond your comfort zone. You may also want to look into an assertive training course. Offer to be on a telephone committee for a fund-raising program or a volunteer agency where you are not personally affected by the response to the calls.

14. *I'm afraid of rejection.* Rejection is an expected part of networking. View each rejection as moving one step closer to your goal. And whatever you do, never, never take rejection personally.

15. *No one understands my real needs.* It is your responsibility to be clearly focused on what it is you want from a networking contact. Prepare a succinct thirty-second presentation or script that describes to your potential contacts exactly what you are seeking. Use this script to practice, practice, practice.

Please feel free to photocopy the list on the next page. Carry it with you to remind yourself that you *can* overcome your networking barriers. Share it with your friends and business associates.

■ Barriers to Networking

1. I don't have any contacts.

2. I don't like having other people solve my problems.

3. It'll appear as if I'm begging.

4. I don't like to use people.

5. I will owe too many favors.

6. I feel uncomfortable networking and I lack confidence.

7. I don't know what to say.

8. I hate cold calls.

9. No one can help me. Why should they?

10. It doesn't work.

11. I don't know how or where to start.

12. I don't have enough time.

13. I'm shy.

14. I'm afraid of rejection.

15. No one understands my real needs.

CHAPTER 5

Networking Etiquette . . . or "Netiquette"

"Be really honest and straightforward in stating your objective when networking—don't misrepresent your reason for seeing someone."

Barry Adamson
President
Murray Axmith & Associates

Every social gathering or business event provides a unique opportunity for you to achieve
your networking goal. Whether it is a company
conference, convention, seminar, book launch,
cocktail party, or association dinner, the success
of your evening can depend on how you behave.
Following and practicing a few basic rules goes a
long way to enhancing your professional image.

Miss Manners and Emily Post would certainly agree that being
considerate and courteous of others' feelings underlies good business etiquette. So, before you head out to exchange business cards,
you may want to consider some of the following guidelines.

1. *Arrive on time or no more than five minutes late for an event.* If you
   arrive too early, you'll have more time to get more nervous.
   Arrive too late and you may feel like you have to play "catch-
   up" or that you're not part of the group at all.

2. *Stand tall, look at people, shake hands, smile.* Enter a room with an
   air of confidence. If there was ever a time to "fake it till you
   make it," it's now! Try looking around like you are looking
   for someone you know, whether you really are or not.

   The last thing you want to project at any networking event is
   awkwardness or uncertainty. Try to remain poised and calm,
   even if you have butterflies the size of the state of Texas. A
   smile can hide a lot of pain and discomfort.

3. *Locate the food table.* Position yourself to meet people. Everyone
   filters towards the buffet table or bar at some point. Position
   yourself conveniently, but be sure not to have your mouth full
   of food. If you do, you won't be able to greet people, let alone
   network with anyone. Remember, impressions count.

4. *Hold your drink in your left hand; shake with your right.* Surely
   you've met people who've had to wipe their wet, cold hand
   on the side of their clothing before they could shake your
   hand. Their hand was still wet and cold though, wasn't it? Try
   wrapping a napkin around the glass you're holding to keep
   your hand dry.

5. *Reintroduce yourself to people you know first.* Start with a familiar face. At least you know you know that person. Don't feel embarrassed about reintroducing yourself, especially in a large group. No one expects you to remember everyone's name. On the other hand, if someone is fumbling with your name, introduce yourself right away and spare that person some embarrassment.

6. *Try to meet as many people as possible.* Don't monopolize any one person for more than ten minutes. If you're having a great conversation with someone, politely excuse yourself and suggest that you touch base later on or arrange a time to get together later in the week. A phone call the next day works too.

7. When it comes to business cards, keep this rule of thumb in mind: *Exchange business cards only after a conversation in which you've established a rapport with the other person.*

8. *Do what you say you will do.* Follow through. You'll lose some credibility if you don't.

9. *Stand.* You can't circulate and be sociable if you're sitting down. Sitting gives the impression that you're tired or can't be bothered to meet people. Stand up and move around.

10. *Don't smoke.* In many parts of North America, smokers are the minority and often there are local ordinances against smoking indoors.

11. *Approach only groups of three or more;* two people may be having a tête-a-tête. Stand on the outside of the group until there is a break in the conversation or until you are acknowledged to join in.

12. *Learn the correct procedure for introducing others.* Etiquette dictates that a younger person is introduced to an older person, and a person of lesser authority is introduced to one of greater authority. Now you just have to remember names and pronounce them correctly!

13. *Don't flirt.* Flirting can be misconstrued; reputations can be made or broken by someone else's perception of you.

14. *Use humor, but avoid sarcasm or telling belittling or off-color jokes.* Humor is an excellent ice breaker, but if you "don't got it, don't flaunt it." People who are nervous often tend to try too hard, talk too loud or too long, show off with sarcasm or by telling off-color jokes. This may be your cue to listen more and talk less.

15. *Listen.* Everyone loves a good listener. Keep your eyes on the speaker, nod to indicate agreement and interest, and ask questions during appropriate breaks. Darting your eyes is rude.

16. *Don't rush the buffet table.* You're at a networking event, not a food fest, so keep your food consumption down. Be remembered for your professional presence, not for your appetite.

17. *Leave when you say you're going to leave.* Ever been asked "Oh, are you still here? I thought you left an hour ago." Embarrassing, isn't it? Leave when you say you're going to leave, and be sure to thank the host before you go.

    Depending on the size of the town or city you live in or near, try to attend at least one new networking function each month. The more networking opportunities you take advantage of, the more comfortable you will become with the rules of "netiquette." You may feel more comfortable taking a friend or business associate with you at first, but as your skills develop and you gain confidence, do try to go it alone. The last thing you need is someone else dragging you down. It could be like taking a new date to a high-school reunion.

■"Netiquette"

1. Arrive on time.

2. Stand tall, look at people, shake hands, smile.

3. Locate the food table. Position yourself to meet people.

4. Hold your drink in your left hand; shake with your right.

5. Reintroduce yourself to people you know first.

6. Meet as many people as possible, but for no more than 10 minutes each.

7. Exchange business cards only after you've established a rapport with another person.

8. Do what you say you will do—follow up.

9. Stand.

10. Don't smoke.

11. Approach only groups of three or more people.

12. Introduce younger people to older, those with less authority to greater authority.

13. Don't flirt.

14. Use humor. Avoid sarcasm or telling belittling or off-color jokes.

15. Listen. Make eye contact and nod. Don't eye dart.

16. Don't rush the buffet table.

17. Leave when you say you're going to leave.

Personal Appearances

Remember, too, that personal appearances count. First impressions are lasting impressions. You don't have to have a lot of money to be neat and clean. Wear a big smile, use moderate or no cologne or after-shave, go easy on the jewelry, and maintain a businesslike posture and demeanor. Remember, you're selling yourself first and foremost.

CHAPTER 6

Improving Your Networking Skills

"My favorite way to network and meet new kinds of people is to do volunteer work. This can be done on weekends and evenings. You'll do good things and meet new people."

Emily Koltnow
Founder of Women
in Networking (WIN)
Co-author of *Congratulations!*
You've Been Fired

How are you doing? Have you been out practicing some of the techniques and procedures we've discussed so far? Good for you! Do you think you could do better? Then you're ready for some fine-tuning.

Like everything else in life, once you've tried something different from the norm a few times, the unfamiliar becomes familiar and what was difficult becomes easy. Networking is no exception. You will find certain ways of doing things that work better than others. Own them, use them, hone them even further, and then share them with others.

You will really feel like your network is working for you when people start coming to you for information or resources. Give yourself as many opportunities as possible to practice and expand your network and you'll be a consummate networker before you know it! Those who put forth the extra effort are the same people who can demand and will receive the lion's share of success in their field.

Here are some tips for improving your networking skills. Follow them and you will "stand like a giraffe in a herd of field mice."

1. Although you are the one asking for advice or information, remember this suggestion: *give more than you get.* You can give by sending thank yous, by passing along articles on topics that would interest your contact, or by referring business to your contact.

2. *Get to know people for who they are, not just for their positions;* that is, get to know the human side of people. Believe it or not, we are not our jobs or our titles. Everyone has unique and interesting things about them that are worth getting to know. Practice striking up conversations that are totally unrelated to work, even if you are at a company function. People love to talk about themselves, so initiate a conversation about a local hero, sports team, or new movie or book. Ask questions.

3. *Follow up on all leads.* You just never know who people know. Who would ever have thought that you could ask a former President of the United States where you could get a good deal on peanuts. It will probably take only a few minutes of your day to call every lead on your list. Even if someone on

the list can't help you out with your present situation, keep that person's name and phone number for future reference. And even if that person isn't able to help you directly, maybe some day you can help others by referring them to that individual.

4. *Report back to those who give you a lead.* Do you ever wonder what happened to "Fred"? The last time you talked to him you gave him a stock tip that should have made him millions. But you haven't heard from him since.

   When someone gives you a lead, call or write to let that person know the outcome, or at least the initial result. On the other hand, you don't need to take your reporting to an extreme, calling every time you are asked to an interview, receive a letter, or have a conversation with someone as the result of the lead. But do report back something.

5. *Don't tell everything to everyone.* Sometimes you can talk too much. If, for example, your networking goal is to make contacts who can give you information so that you can corner a business deal, you don't want to reveal any more information than you have to. If you provide too many details about the deal, you may tip your hand and give someone else an opportunity to close on the deal before you do.

6. *Ask for exactly what you need.* Put together a precise, thirty-second blurb about what you are seeking. If your contacts need more information, they'll ask.

   You have to at least sound like you know what you want. After all, if you don't know, you can't expect others to know. And if they don't know, then they can't keep their eyes and ears open for you.

7. *Keep your word.* Do what you say you will do. If you tell someone you'll have some information ready by a certain date, make sure that you do. There's no room for procrastination when it affects others' needs. Your professional reputation could be at stake.

8. *Don't immediately reject advice.* Even if you've already tried every single idea someone suggests to you, politely accept the

information anyway. Dismiss it later if you want to. Or, if some of the ideas you're offered seem outlandish or off the wall, hold on to them for another time. You never know when you or someone else may be able to use them. Or, you may be able to slightly modify the suggestion to make it workable.

9. *Don't expect your network to function as the "be all and end all."* Once you've passed the word around about what it is you need, keep moving. Utilize other avenues besides your network to work for you. Read books and newspapers, trade publications (both the articles and the advertisements), attend the meetings and conventions of clubs or organizations that enhance your personal and professional interests, and listen more than you speak.

10. *Make networking a habit.* Adopt it as a way of life. Experts say that to acquire a new habit or to change an old one, you must practice it for 21 days in a row and then you will own it. No excuses, just do it!

■ Improving Your Networking Skills

1. Try to give more than you get.

2. Get to know people for who they are, not just for their positions.

3. Follow up on all leads.

4. Report back to those who give you a lead.

5. Don't tell everything to everyone.

6. Ask for exactly what you need. Be focused and succinct in your message.

7. Keep your word.

8. Don't immediately reject advice.

9. Don't expect your network to function as the "be all and end all."

10. Make networking a habit.

CHAPTER 7

The Advice Call

"The Advice Call can help people gain access to business people, executives, politicians, managers, and entrepreneurs."

Bill Nolan
Networker Extraordinaire and
Advice Call Perfectionist

(This chapter is written in memory of Bill Nolan, management consultant and Director of The Institute for Marketing Professional Services in Toronto.)

The Advice Call is a technique that gives you access to the people you need to meet to achieve your goals. The sole purpose of the Advice Call is to gain expert advice from people who are successful in the areas you are interested in. Properly made, each Advice Call will benefit you in at least five ways:

1. You will receive a wealth of advice from successful people.
2. You will sharpen your interview skills.
3. Rather than "going it alone," seeking positive interaction with people you perceive as winners can help you face your challenges.
4. The Advice Call allows you to control the interview session. Try to listen 70 percent of the time and talk only 30 percent. The key is to ask precise, focused questions based on your needs and interests so that during the 70 percent of time you spend listening, you are receiving the information you really need.
5. The Advice Call can lead to referrals and further interviews. Always ask your contact for the names of two or three other people who could further your fact-finding mission. Also be sure to ask whether you can use your contact's name as a reference.

Getting Started

If you are starting from scratch—that is, without any contacts or leads—begin the process with research. Go to the library to investigate business journals and industry-specific publications. If, for example, you want to know which new or used cars are recommended for the year, start by reading *Lemon-Aid,* a consumer publication that offers information for people wanting to purchase automobiles. Then head out to dealerships that sell the recommended models and makes.

Or, if you need to meet people, consider conducting your first interviews with people you know and trust, but who are knowledgeable in the area you are interested in—perhaps business cohorts, friends, or acquaintances. When you request an interview with them, be as specific as possible about what you are trying to accomplish so you don't waste either your time or theirs. Choose people you feel can give you some valuable advice and information— decision makers or people who are experts in that particular area.

Getting Through on the Phone

 When you call your contact to schedule an interview, you may encounter a few obstacles. In order to get through, you must be polite, firm, confident, and persistent—and, of course, prepared. The secretary who screens your calls is only doing a job. He or she doesn't know you and is not personally out to make your life difficult. Form an alliance with this person. You may be speaking to him or her several more times before you actually connect with your contact.

You:	"Hello. May I speak to (name of your contact), please?"
Secretary:	"He's busy (or unavailable) right now. Can I help you?"
You:	(*Ahhh!! Remember to relax.*) "No, thank you. It's a personal *matter*" or "It's a technical *matter*." (Be sure to use the word *matter*.)

Ask when your contact is expected to return, and make a note to call back. Consider calling early in the morning before anyone else has arrived or later in the day, after 5:00 p.m., when executives are likely to answer their own phones. Or you may try calling just before noon when your contact is probably in the office getting ready to leave for lunch.

When you have a referral, be sure to use it. A referral is a guaranteed door opener.

Secretary:	"May I say who's calling?"
You:	"This is Jane Doe. John Smith referred me to (name of your contact)."

You might also mention that you are calling long distance. Doing so sometimes gives your call a sense of urgency.

Don't leave your telephone number if your contact is not in. Once you give away your number, you give away your control. If, however, you've been playing telephone tag all day and will be at your desk or phone expecting the call, *and you have a referral*, you might consider leaving your number. Otherwise, you could wait forever for the contact to return your call or you may miss the call when it does come in.

The Script

Once you have your contact on the phone, your call will probably go something like this:

> "(Name of contact), my name is (your name). I was speaking to (name of referral) recently, and your name came up as someone who may be able to help me. I am calling professionals such as yourself in the (area of interest) industry to seek advice. When could we get together for about twenty minutes? Would (day of week) morning or (day of week) afternoon be better?"

If your contact is a little confused about the nature of your call, reiterate that you want to gain from his or her knowledge and experience. You may want to point out that you *are not selling anything or looking for a job* and that you will not stay for more than twenty minutes. (Be sure to stick to your word. Remember, your professional reputation is at stake. Do what you say you will do.)

To secure an appointment, use a sales technique called *assuming the close*. Ask: "Would Monday morning or Tuesday afternoon be better?" When you use this technique, you'll find that your contacts will be so intent on looking in their date books to firm up a date that they forget it is the meeting itself they should be agreeing to first, not the date.

Try not to let your contact interview you over the telephone. If you must provide some information about your background and situation, do so briefly. But remember: Get back to the issue of when you and your contact can meet.

Once you've secured an appointment, repeat the date and time to your contact, leave your phone number, and get off the phone. You can get the address and directions from the receptionist or secretary later. Some people will argue that you shouldn't leave your phone number so your contact can't cancel the appointment. Well, there's nothing worse than getting primed for an interview and driving halfway across town in rush-hour traffic only to find that your contact has the flu but couldn't reach you to cancel. Think about it.

Please understand that if your contact doesn't agree to see you, that that person may truly be too busy. Or maybe your contact believes that he or she can't help you and suggests that you meet instead with someone else in the organization. If this is the case, qualify your contact's recommendation by ensuring that the referral has expertise in the area. Under no circumstances should you agree to talk to anyone in the human resources or personnel department, unless, of course, you are looking for a job or information in that department.

The Information Interview

Never lose track of the purpose of your meeting: to gain information or to get advice from a professional. If you are indeed looking for work, the worst faux pas you can commit is to ask for a job rather than the information or advice you initially requested.

Conduct this meeting—the Information Interview—like any other business appointment. Greet your contact with a firm handshake, make direct eye contact, and smile. Thank him or her for agreeing to take the time to see you. Once you are comfortable, begin to establish control by getting right to the point. You have invited yourself into this person's office, so be prepared and take control.

Begin by giving your contact an overview of your research or your situation to this point. Offer a brief synopsis of your background and your goal as it pertains to the purpose of the meeting. This information should be well-prepared and rehearsed, taking no more than two minutes to deliver. Keep your sentences short. Don't include dates; use lengths of time instead:

> "I worked for an insurance company for four years and took courses all along that allowed me to move into a more progressive department within the company."

Then say:

> "Put yourself in my shoes. With that background, what would your advice to me be?"

Be more specific about your plans as the meeting progresses:

> "One of the things I'm considering is doing some volunteer work to sharpen my skills. What are your thoughts on that?"

Be deliberately open-minded and listen carefully to your contact's answer. You may be given advice that you will be able to use for the rest of your life. Don't argue with or dispute the suggestions your contact offers. Doing so will only make your contact less willing to make further suggestions.

Remember to stick to the twenty-minute time limit. To prove how well-intentioned you are, book your appointment for ten past the hour or twenty minutes to the hour. Check your watch when you go into the meeting and make a point of closing the meeting on time. Keep your word. If you are asked to stay longer, refuse the first time. If your contact is adamant that it's okay, accept graciously and stay for no more than an hour.

If you are conducting an Advice Call or an Informational Interview for the purpose of networking for a job, never, never, never take your resume with you. Certainly never offer it to your contact. Presenting your resume makes it look like you are there to ask for a job, which you promised you would not do! If your contact does ask for your resume, offer to mail a copy. Doing so will put your name back in your contact's thoughts a few days later, when the resume arrives in the mail.

If your Advice Call doesn't yield immediate results, don't be discouraged. Your call may pay off later in ways you didn't anticipate. Consider the results of Cynthia's Advice Call:

Cynthia S. was a very proactive young job seeker who wanted to make the switch from sales to marketing. She networked her way into an Informational Interview with a vice president for a supplier to Pepsi Cola. He was impressed with Cynthia and asked for her resume, mentioning that he didn't have any opportunities but would like to keep her in mind.

After the interview, Cynthia sent her resume to him, along with a thank you letter. Several days later she received a phone call from a brand manager at Pepsi, Toronto, who asked her to come in for an interview for a six-month contract position. Impressed with Cynthia, her first contact had forwarded her resume to Pepsi thinking there might be something for her there. And there was! Seventeen months later, Cynthia was still working for Pepsi, gaining valuable marketing experience from an international corporation—all because she took the initiative to get out there and make those calls!

Finally, send a thank you letter or card within thirty-six hours of your appointment. As Susan RoAne writes in *How to Work a Room,* "the handwritten note . . . reflects personal care, thought, and time expended." But remember this: If you have indecipherable handwriting, type your letter.

Use the thank you note to review a few of the meeting's highlights. Above all, express appreciation for your contact's time and expertise. Also mention how you're progressing with any referrals your contact gave you:

> "I spoke to Mrs. Brown, the product manager you referred me to, and we are meeting next week."

This may also be your opportunity to *exchange:*

> "As a follow-up to our conversation about benchmarking new R & D products in the sports industry, I've enclosed an article I thought you might be interested in."

The Advice Call has worked for thousands of people—the challenge is to get it to work for you!

CHAPTER 8

Expanding Your Network–And Making It Work for You

"If you want to be a networker, you have to be a broadcaster."

Brad L. Clarke
President
Clarke, Hammett
and Associates

By now, you should know of at least three ways to develop a network:

1. Contacting people you already know (your contact network)
2. Attending conferences and seminars, taking courses, attending association meetings, doing volunteer work
3. Cold calling people you have researched on your own through trade journals, directories, and newspaper or magazine articles

Now you are ready to develop your network even further. To start, go back to Exercise 4 and review the contacts you listed. Now add another 100 or 150 names to your list. Keep in mind that everyone knows between 100 and 1,000 people on a personal, social, or business basis. Did you remember to include former teachers or students, parents of friends, ex-spouses?

Your existing network will work for you right away, so start with it. Ask for a referral from each person you speak to or meet with. Before you know it, you will be besieged with names. And by this time, you should have acquired the confidence to surge ahead and call these people who are less familiar to you.

Decide which of these people could help you achieve the networking goals you set for yourself in Exercise 1. Who could best provide you with the information or resources you need? Then consider which of those people you will feel most comfortable contacting first. It takes about two or three network contacts to generate a solid information lead. Make a point to contact those people within the next week.

Use Exercise 5 to help you plan your contacts.

> Knowing how to network — how to ask for help and how to give it — is a survival skill in today's workplace."
>
> Janis Foord Kirk
> *Surviving the Upheaval in Your Workplace*

▇ EXERCISE 5:
Planning Your Networking Contacts

1. This week I am prepared to:

   phone my lawyer and real estate agent

   _____

   _____

   _____

   _____

2. By the end of the month I will be ready to:

   talk to the people in my cooking class

   _____

   _____

   _____

3. The areas I still need to work on are:

   meeting the neighbors

   _____

   _____

   _____

   _____

Group Networking

Another way to expand your network is to take advantage of group networking activities. Group networking is a totally empowering and involved networking experience. Look for business card exchanges, dinner or luncheon meetings, company cocktail parties, association or club meetings, school events, volunteer work, self-help groups, stockholder annual meetings, and reunions. Scan the newspaper or public bulletin boards for more ideas. Remember to keep a journal and/or an information gathering report (see page 55) to record who you meet when and where as well as some personal background on each new contact.

Here are some of the group networking opportunities that exist:

1. *Brainstorming groups.* Aside from joining associations affiliated with your job or hobby, watch for groups such as APEX in Toronto that are created to give people the opportunity to exchange ideas and to offer support. The purpose of APEX, for example, is "to create a positive, inspiring, friendly, growth-fostering environment where people can get to know each other and share their dreams and goals, both personally and professionally." Groups such as APEX typically meet once or twice a month, sometimes over a buffet dinner. Members give and receive ideas, information, business referrals, motivation, support, and friendship. At these types of networking gatherings, be sure to bring business cards, brochures, resumes, a list of your goals, and, above all, an open mind!

   If you don't know of such a group in your area, start one of your own! Think of five people you've always wanted to sit across the table from during dinner. Create your own opportunity. Call those people and invite them to gather for an informal exchange of ideas.

2. *Masterminding.* Mastermind groups are starting up all over. They consist of about five groups of eight like-minded individuals who meet once a week for two or three hours. Each person in the group gets five minutes to outline his or her problem or concern and then notes the suggestions of others in the group. This problem-solving period lasts fifteen

minutes. During this time, group members are not allowed to dispute any recommendation. The object is to brainstorm. This process continues around the table until each person in the group has had a turn.

Later, each person picks and chooses which suggestions to follow. There is no obligation to make helpful people feel good by following up on their suggestions. But you must be totally committed to achieving your goal and to attending each and every meeting. Everyone reports back the following week as to the outcome of the suggestions.

3. *Barn raising.* In their book *Wishcraft*, Barbara Sher and Annie Gottlieb talk about "success teams," which are very similar to masterminding groups. Sher advocates group brainstorming through a barn-raising get-together. Start by inviting a few of your close friends. Ask each of them to bring someone interesting and, of course, something good to eat and drink. You may start and end with socializing, but in the middle it's got to be business, with everyone's attention focused on the problem at hand.

   For barn raising to be effective, Sher suggests two important rules:
   1. Be as specific as possible about what you need, such as a used car for less than $500 or a contact in the recording industry.
   2. Always ask for the most specific information you can get (names, addresses, book titles, etc.).

   As with any networking process, follow through and report back to the individuals who gave you the leads or resources.

Computer Networking

Did you ever have a pen pal when you were a kid? Ever listen to those raspy, haunting voices from around the world over your dad's ham radio? These were the original long-distance means of network communication.

Well, we've come a million technological miles in the way we communicate since pen pals and ham radios. Today a book on networking would hardly be complete without some mention of networking through computers. Keep in mind that networking is an exchange of information or resources, which is exactly what takes place in various forms between thousands of computer communicators around the world. Here are a few of the ways people use computers to network everyday:

1. *Electronic mail or e-mail.* When you don't need to talk to someone right here and now, computer e-mail is one of the most inexpensive, convenient, and effective ways to communicate with anyone, anywhere. Electronic mail simply consists of messages that one person sends to another person or several people via computer.

   The advantages of e-mail are numerous. The person receiving the message does not need to be at his or her computer when messages are sent. Further, the recipient isn't interrupted to receive messages. Messages are saved until the receiver chooses to read them. Further, the receiver may choose to print the messages, save them to disk, or forward them to others.

2. *Bulletin Board Services (BBS).* A BBS is a computer that has been programmed to answer the telephone. Simply put, BBSs allow you to communicate with others through your computer over the telephone line.

   Most BBSs are created and run by computer hobbyists who have an interest in a particular area. The BBS allows others with similar interests to exchange messages or to publish information. (Remember, the key to any networking experience is *exchange.*)

   To use a bulletin board, you need a computer terminal or personal computer containing a modem and a telephone line.

3. *On-line services.* Using your personal computer, a modem, and the appropriate software you can literally turn your computer into a communications center. Among their many features, these on-line services allow subscribers access to news services; the latest sports, financial, and weather information; events calendars; encyclopedias; games and entertainment; travel and shopping services; and information from national experts on organizing, managing, and promoting a business.

4. *Internet.* Internet is a huge network of networks. It connects over ten million people around the world through computers in universities, research laboratories, and commercial and military sites. As James MacFarlane mentions in his article "Enter the Internet," no other technology rings truer to the notion of global village than the Internet network.

Computers allow extremely powerful and far-reaching networking opportunities. You have seen what an incredible resource you can become when networking person to person. Just imagine the information you'll have at your fingertips when you delve into the world of computer networking.

CHAPTER 9

Organizing Your Network

"Organization is the foundation of networking and there are many different ways. Everyone has her own ideas of how to be organized; ask around."

Anne Boe
Is Your "Net" Working?

You can spend hours developing new contacts and leads every week, but the time you spend doing so won't be worth a thing unless you organize that information so that you can access it quickly and easily. You will need a system and the proper tools for organizing your contacts, telephone numbers, where and when you met, perhaps a description of what your contacts look like, where they fit into your goals, and follow-up activities.

The extent to which you organize yourself will determine how effectively your network ultimately works for you. Using index cards, spiral notebooks, or time-saving organizers can help you keep track of your information effectively and efficiently. Set up your files to include the following information:

- Name of contact
- Address and phone number of contact
- Where you met and the date
- A physical description or outstanding feature of your contact
- The contact's occupation or affiliation
- Date last contacted
- Date that thank you letter or correspondence was sent
- Any referrals suggested
- Additional notes

Information Gathering Report

After each of your meetings or calls, complete an information gathering report similar to the one on the next page. Consider custom designing the report to complement the organizational tools you use to keep track of your networking data. For example, the report form that follows could easily be copied and filed in a three-ring binder. Or it could be used as a model for creating the fields in a database record if you use a computer to store your networking information.

Information Gathering Report
Sample

Date _____

Person _____ Title _____

Organization _____

Address _____

_____

_____

Phone _____

Referred by _____

Industry/Subject _____

Date thank you sent _____

1. What did you learn about your contact? _____

_____

2. What did you learn about this industry/topic area? _____

_____

3. What opinions did your contact have? _____

_____

4. What suggestions did your contact make? _____

_____

5. Some of my positive impressions are _____

_____

6. Some of my negative impressions are _____

_____

7. Referrals: name, title, function, background _____

_____

8. Things I would do differently next time _____

_____

9. Comments _____

_____

Planning Calendar

You will need a calendar with space that allows you to plan ahead for at least six months. For each contact you keep in touch with, enter the next call date in your planning calendar, whether that appointment is one week, three months, or six months away. Check your calendar daily, weekly, and monthly so you know which appointments are coming up.

Business Cards

Whether you are a recent graduate looking for a job, a sales representative sniffing out sales leads, or a secretary selling handicrafts, business cards are a must! They should represent you in the most professional light possible, reflecting to some extent your individuality. They should include your name, telephone, and address, as well as your position, industry, trade, or interest. If you have more than one business, use a separate card for each one. A law clerk who is doing graphics work on the side would have a different card for her part-time business. She wouldn't use the same card she uses in her position as a law clerk. The same is true of a public speaker who also designs and knits unique sweaters.

The Answering Machine

It is no longer considered an imposition for a caller to leave a message on an answering machine. Being able to leave a detailed message is an enormous time saver and convenience for both the caller and the receiver. Make sure the message you leave provides the receiver with the information he or she will need to call you back.

Microcassette Recorder

Ideas often come at the most inconvenient times. For those times when it's just not convenient to write something down, a portable, pocket-sized tape recorder comes in handy. They are inexpensive, easy to use, and travel easily in your pocket, briefcase, or purse.

The Computer

If you have access to a computer, either at home or at work, the ultimate recording system is an up-to-date database of all the contacts you have acquired. There are several quality database programs on the market.

Computer Notebook

These little wonders are springing up in boardrooms, at the beach, and at networking meetings all around the country. They're still a bit pricey, but they go anywhere and store an incredible amount of information. Be sure to get one that allows you to back up your data onto a diskette because they do go down once in a while. If that happens, you'll lose hundreds of pieces of often irretrievable data.

Stationery

Even if you don't require personalized letterhead and envelopes, it's always a nice touch to use thank you cards or note cards personalized with your name or initials engraved or embossed on the front. If you do have matching stationery, the writing paper and envelope paper should match and be of watermark quality, or the best you can afford.

Carrying Case

A nice carrying case or portfolio gives you a professional image and sends out the message that you are organized and serious about your goals. A carrying case is almost a necessity for men because they do not have the advantage of carrying a purse.

Writing Implements

Carry a working pen or pencil with you at all times. And remember, the quality of your pen says a great deal about you. Chances are you won't chew on the end of a good metal pen like you might on a plastic disposable.

Now, take a few minutes to assess whether you have the tools you need to organize your networking contacts.

■ EXERCISE 6:

Networking Tools Inventory

The networking tools I have in my possession are:

1. _____

2. _____

3. _____

4. _____

5. _____

The networking tools I need to acquire are:

1. _____

2. _____

3. _____

4. _____

5. _____

Be focused!

Have fun!

Stretch and grow!

Share your wisdom!

Happy Networking!

OOH AHH!

Use this page to write down any great (or "Ooh Ahh") networking ideas that you think of.

Bibliography and Suggested Reading

Barnes, Carolyn, and Marilyn Manning. *Professional Excellence for Secretaries*. Los Altos, CA: Crisp, 1988.

Boe, Anne. *Is Your "Net" Working?: A Complete Guide to Building Contacts and Career Visibility*. New York: Wiley, 1989.

Dudley, Denise M. *Every Woman's Guide to Career Success*. Mission, KS: SkillPath Publications, 1991.

Foord Kirk, Janis. *Surviving the Upheaval in Your Workplace*. Kirkfoord Communications, 1992.

Koltnow, Emily, and Lynne S. Dumas. *Congratulations! You've Been Fired: Sound Advice for Women Who've Been Terminated, Pink-Slipped, Downsized, or Otherwise Unemployed*. New York: Fawcett Columbine, 1990.

Lipnack, Jessica, and Jeffrey Stamps. *The Networking Book: People Connecting With People*. New York: Routledge & Kegan Paul, 1986.

Mackay, Harvey. *Swim With the Sharks Without Being Eaten Alive: Outsell, Outmanage, Outmotivate and Outnegotiate Your Competition*. New York: Morrow, 1988.

Putnam, Anthony O. *Marketing Your Services: A Step-by-Step Guide for Small Businesses and Professionals*. New York: Wiley, 1990.

Raye-Johnson, Venda. *Effective Networking*. Los Altos, CA: Crisp, 1990.

RoAne, Susan. *How to Work a Room: A Guide to Successfully Managing the Mingling*. New York: Shapolsky Publishers, 1988.

Sher, Barbara, and Annie Gottlieb. *Wishcraft: How to Get What You Really Want*. New York: Viking Press, 1979.

Sturman, Gerald M. *The Career Discovery Project*. New York: Doubleday, 1993.

Vilas, Donna, and Sandy Vilas. *Power Networking: 55 Secrets for Personal and Professional Success*. Austin, TX: MountainHarbour Publications, 1992.

Available From SkillPath Publications

Self-Study Sourcebooks

The Business and Technical Writer's Guide *by Robert McGraw*

Aim First: Get Focused and Fired Up to Follow Through on Your Goals *by Lee T. Silber*

Climbing the Corporate Ladder: What You Need to Know and Do to Be a Promotable Person *by Barbara Pachter and Marjorie Brody*

Coping With Supervisory Nightmares: 12 Common Nightmares of Leadership and What You Can Do About Them *by Michael and Deborah Singer Dobson*

Defeating Procrastination: 52 Fail-Safe Tips for Keeping Time on Your Side *by Marlene Caroselli, Ed.D.*

Discovering Your Purpose *by Ivy Haley*

Going for the Gold: Winning the Gold Medal for Financial Independence *by Lesley D. Bissett, CFP*

Having Something to Say When You Have to Say Something: The Art of Organizing Your Presentation *by Randy Horn*

Info-Flood: How to Swim in a Sea of Information Without Going Under *by Marlene Caroselli, Ed.D.*

The Innovative Secretary *by Marlene Caroselli, Ed.D.*

Letters & Memos: Just Like That! *by Dave Davies*

Mastering the Art of Communication: Your Keys to Developing a More Effective Personal Style *by Michelle Fairfield Poley*

Organized for Success! 95 Tips for Taking Control of Your Time, Your Space, and Your Life *by Nanci McGraw*

A Passion to Lead! How to Develop Your Natural Leadership Ability *by Michael Plumstead*

P.E.R.S.U.A.D.E.: Communication Strategies That Move People to Action *by Marlene Caroselli, Ed.D.*

Productivity Power: 250 Great Ideas for Being More Productive *by Jim Temme*

Promoting Yourself: 50 Ways to Increase Your Prestige, Power, and Paycheck *by Marlene Caroselli, Ed.D.*

Proof Positive: How to Find Errors Before They Embarrass You *by Karen L. Anderson*

Risk-Taking: 50 Ways to Turn Risks Into Rewards *by Marlene Caroselli, Ed.D. and David Harris*

Speak Up and Stand Out: How to Make Effective Presentations *by Nanci McGraw*

Stress Control: How You Can Find Relief From Life's Daily Stress *by Steve Bell*

Total Quality Customer Service: How to Make It Your Way of Life *by Jim Temme*

Write It Right! A Guide for Clear and Correct Writing *by Richard Andersen and Helene Hinis*

Your Total Communication Image *by Janet Signe Olson, Ph.D.*

Handbooks

The ABC's of Empowered Teams: Building Blocks for Success *by Mark Towers*

Assert Yourself! Developing Power-Packed Communication Skills to Make Your Points Clearly, Confidently, and Persuasively *by Lisa Contini*

Breaking the Ice: How to Improve Your On-the-Spot Communication Skills
by Deborah Shouse

The Care and Keeping of Customers: A Treasury of Facts, Tips, and Proven Techniques for Keeping Your Customers Coming BACK! *by Roy Lantz*

Challenging Change: Five Steps for Dealing With Change *by Holly DeForest and Mary Steinberg*

Dynamic Delegation: A Manager's Guide for Active Empowerment *by Mark Towers*

Every Woman's Guide to Career Success *by Denise M. Dudley*

Exploring Personality Styles: A Guide for Better Understanding Yourself and Your Colleagues *by Michael Dobson*

Grammar? No Problem! *by Dave Davies*

Great Openings and Closings: 28 Ways to Launch and Land Your Presentations With Punch, Power, and Pizazz *by Mari Pat Varga*

Hiring and Firing: What Every Manager Needs to Know *by Marlene Caroselli, Ed.D. with Laura Wyeth, Ms.Ed.*

How to Be a More Effective Group Communicator: Finding Your Role and Boosting Your Confidence in Group Situations *by Deborah Shouse*

How to Deal With Difficult People *by Paul Friedman*

Learning to Laugh at Work: The Power of Humor in the Workplace
by Robert McGraw

Making Your Mark: How to Develop a Personal Marketing Plan for Becoming More Visible and More Appreciated at Work *by Deborah Shouse*

Meetings That Work *by Marlene Caroselli, Ed.D.*

The Mentoring Advantage: How to Help Your Career Soar to New Heights
by Pam Grout

Minding Your Business Manners: Etiquette Tips for Presenting Yourself Professionally in Every Business Situation *by Marjorie Brody and Barbara Pachter*

Misspeller's Guide *by Joel and Ruth Schroeder*

Motivation in the Workplace: How to Motivate Workers to Peak Performance and Productivity *by Barbara Fielder*

NameTags Plus: Games You Can Play When People Don't Know What to Say
by Deborah Shouse

Networking: How to Creatively Tap Your People Resources *by Colleen Clarke*

New & Improved! 25 Ways to Be More Creative and More Effective *by Pam Grout*

Power Write! A Practical Guide to Words That Work *by Helene Hinis*

The Power of Positivity: Eighty ways to energize your life *by Joel and Ruth Schroeder*

Putting Anger to Work For You *by Ruth and Joel Schroeder*

Reinventing Your Self: 28 Strategies for Coping With Change *by Mark Towers*

Saying "No" to Negativity: How to Manage Negativity in Yourself, Your Boss, and Your Co-Workers *by Zoie Kaye*

The Supervisor's Guide: The Everyday Guide to Coordinating People and Tasks
by Jerry Brown and Denise Dudley, Ph.D.

Taking Charge: A Personal Guide to Managing Projects and Priorities
by Michal E. Feder

Treasure Hunt: 10 Stepping Stones to a New and More Confident You! *by Pam Grout*

A Winning Attitude: How to Develop Your Most Important Asset!
by Michelle Fairfield Poley

For more information, call 1-800-873-7545.

Notes

Notes